Building Utopia

FUTURING GUIDEBOOK

BUILDINGUTOPIADECK.COM

Welcome

This book is part of a toolkit for radical Afrofuturist speculation, and was created to help guide you through the process of envisioning equitable futures for yourself and your community.

This kit was designed with the intention of encouraging design with, by and for communities not often represented in the design industry and should be used by and alongside them.

Whether you seek community-centered design inspiration or a container for your ideas, feel free to use this book as a space to house your visions for the future.

Be as creative as you want, this is your space!

RADICAL FUTURING

This workbook is intended to be a resource for:

➤ Imagining futures that are equitable for all and explore possibilities beyond our present-day limitations.

➤ Creating solutions with people who are invested in co-designing better futures.

➤ Drawing from work done in the past and present to see what we can yield in the future.

➤ Considering how the future might be reshaped and the steps needed to get there.

➤ Approaching visions for the future that centers Black diasporic people and values joy, liberation and community building.

Art by: Renato Moll

WHAT IS AFROFUTURISM?

The term 'Afrofuturism' was coined by Mark Dery in 1994 and describes a branch of speculative fiction created by and featuring people of African descent. The genre widened the scope of popular science fiction and can both illuminate engagements in race in present-day social contexts and envison futures that incorporate Black aesthetic and possibilities.

"**Afrofuturism** is a way of imagining possible futures through a Black cultural lens. "

LaFleur, I., Visual Aesthetics of Afrofuturism, TEDx Fort Greene Salon, YouTube, September 25, 2011

How to Use This Toolkit

The Building Utopia toolkit was designed to help you consider more radical visions for your future and the community around you. Each card deck will help you frame current aspects or elements of the future you want to envision. This guidebook is set up to help you get familiar with the card decks, learn about a few design methods that may be new to you, and practice radical futures thinking. Throughout this guidebook we have provided space and prompts for you to envision different futures.

Here is a breakdown of what you'll find in the Guidebook. Go in order or skip around. The choice is yours!

Get to Know the Card Decks: pages 6- 13

Prompts for Speculation: page 16-24

Design Methods to Try: pages 25-30

Radical Futures Thinking: pages 31-38

Certain pages of this guidebook may have a card icon on them in the upper-right corner like the ones below. If you see one, these are suggesred decks that may help you think through the prompts.

We've designed the Building Utopia Toolkit to be used in many ways, allowing you to choose what combination of cards and ideation activities best fit your group and the purpose of your gathering.

Here is one example of how the cards can be ordered.

First, the group picks a Topic card. If the group does not yet have a topic area they would like to address, this card can be drawn randomly or voted on.

Next, the group turns over a card from the Forecasting deck. All future questions will be asked as if the group is designing in this time period.

Then, the group turns over a card from the **Liberation** deck and can take turns sharing their answer to the question on the card.

After, a Methods card is drawn to determine a method you can use to show how your future solution might look.

If you need solution prompts, look for a Tools card to get inspiration for possible categories.

If none of the Topics or Tools are fitting, you can swap in a **Blank** card and fill that out with your own input. Keep in mind that while this is the order the cards are typically used, you know your community best, and can substitute or rearrange the cards to suit your needs.

Examples

"My community already has topics to address"

"The solutions here won't work for us/we came up with a new solution category"

"We just want to identify our shared values"

TOPICS

BLACK JOY

What is Black joy?

Black joy as a form of resistence is the idea that it is vital that even amidst oppression, past or present, Black people can continue to live and enjoy living.

How is Black joy found in your time?

Use this deck to see what challenges and strengths in your community might be addressed or shaped by design solutions. How can we amplify voices that often go unheard when discussing these challenges and strengths?

Ideas for Use

With a group, lay out all the cards and collectively identify 2-3 topics that are particularly meaningful.

-or-

Shuffle the cards and pick the first card in the deck. Consider how it might impact your community or the communities of others.

LIBERATION

Use these cards to consider the ways you and your community can live liberated lives. How do your values impact the solutions you choose in a liberated world?

Ideas for Use

Use the cards as journal prompts, considering how they may influence your visions for the future.

-or-

Pick a Liberation card to discuss with your community collective.

-or-

In a group, pick cards that resonate with each individual and share your responses to the prompts.

FORECASTING

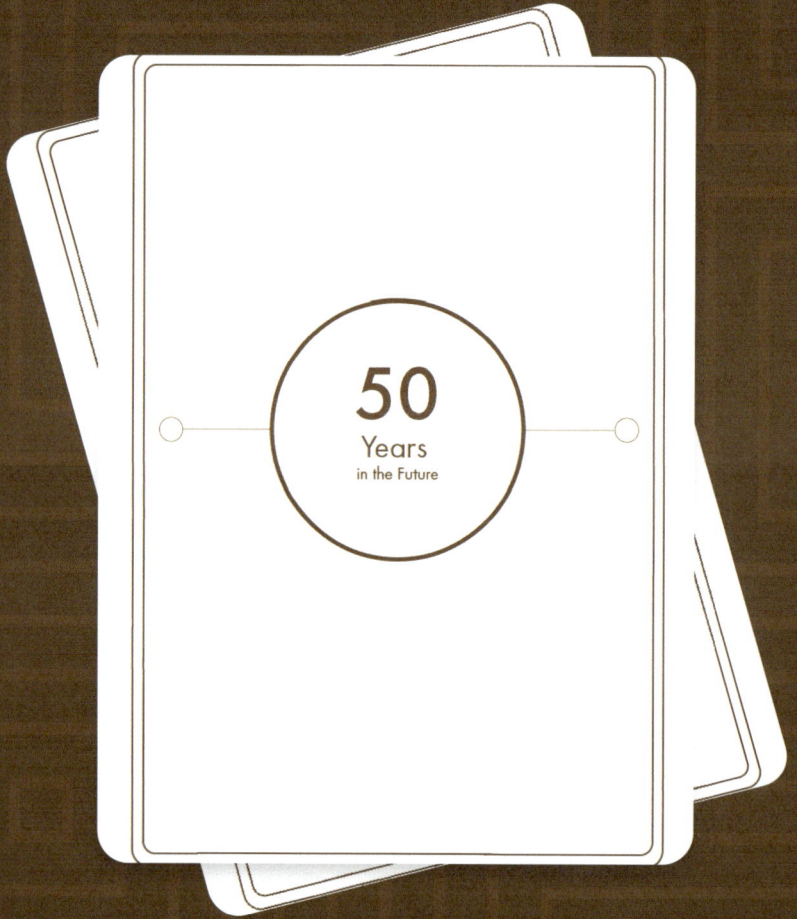

Set a time in which to speculate using these cards. Do you want to consider the future, examine what solutions came before, or see what can be done in the here and now?

Ideas for Use

Pick a date in the future and consider what it will be like, and how change will be brought about.

-or-

Create a design timeline using cards from the past, present, and future to consider how solutions have shaped your community.

-or-

Set goals for the present and the future, near and far.

METHODS

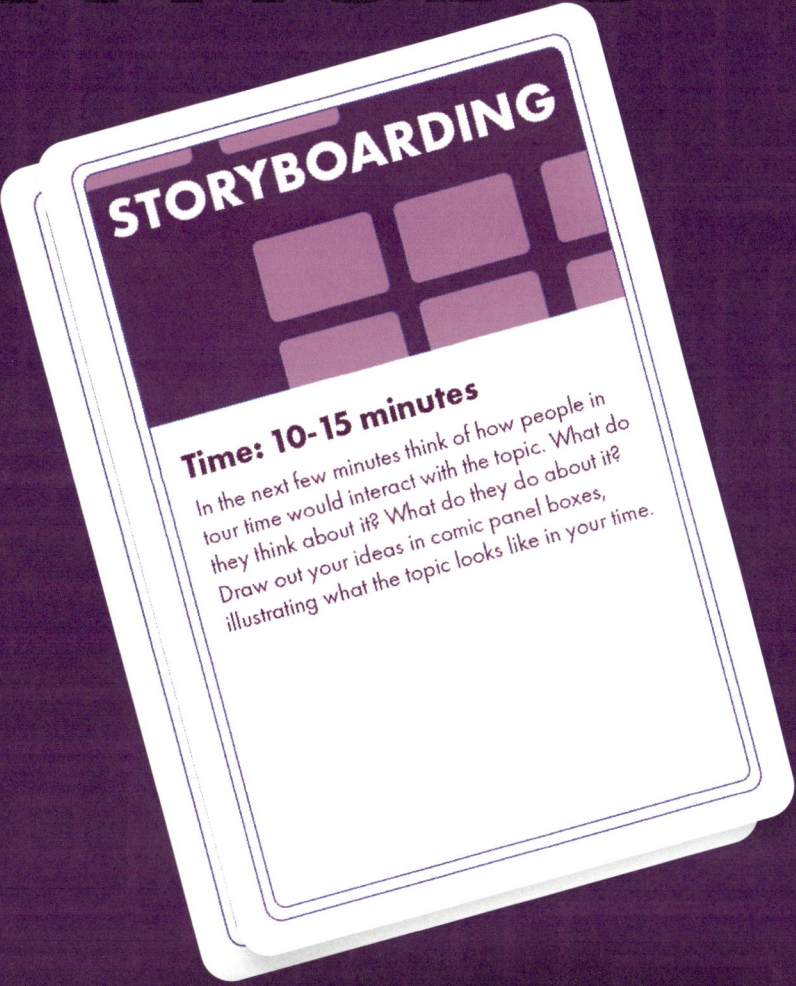

STORYBOARDING

Time: 10-15 minutes

In the next few minutes think of how people in your time would interact with the topic. What do they think about it? What do they do about it? Draw out your ideas in comic panel boxes, illustrating what the topic looks like in your time.

Put your ideas to paper. These design exercises can be used to guide your speculation process and share visions for the future that are informed by the ongoing work from the past and present.

Ideas for Use

Pick a method to be used in a workshop setting.
-or-
Consult with the Topics and Liberation decks, then pick the Method Card that would best fit your needs to vision a solution.
-or-
Choose a random card from this deck and see if it helps you find a new way to address your Topic or reach your vision for Liberation.

TOOLS & SOLUTIONS

The Tools & Solutions cards offer opportunities to consider new or existing ways that joy, liberation, and community building might be encouraged in the future.

Ideas for Use

Pick three tools to see how they might be used to build solutions for your community.

-or-

Pick a random tool and see how you might use it as a future solution for your Topic.

OPEN CARDS

TITLE: _____

Description:

_____

_____

_____

_____

Examples

_____

_____

The ideas and prompts in this deck are not where speculation begins or ends. Use these cards to bring in your own perspectives and find solutions that resonate within your community.

Ideas for Use

Bring in topics, methods, tools or liberation questions you would like to see when you speculate.

-or-

Draw, paint, or collage over the cards to illustrate your ideas.

-or-

Ask others what ideas they would like to add to any of the decks.

When to Use These Cards

Some cards and decks may be more appropriate than others depending on where you are in your design process. Below are 4 stages in which these cards can be used. Take some time to consider what stage you are in and use methods and liberation cards with corresponding numbers.

Planning

In the planning stage, problems or opportunities are defined and communities outline guiding values. You may still be identifying broad topics to address in discussions or by surveying people involved.

1

Exploration

In this stage, we explore opportunities for design. This might involve talking with community members or looking at information gathered in the planning stage to determine what will be needed in a design solution.

2

Building

In this stage, testable prototypes are made to represent what designs will look like in the future. These can be altered or built upon during the design process.

3

Execution and Evaluation

After a design is applied, it is important to see whether it brings the desired outcomes or what may be needed to improve upon it. In this stage the design is evaluated.

4

WHAT IS COMMUNITY DESIGN?

Picture by Andrea Piacquadio

Community design is a process that involves all community stakeholders as contributors, recognizing the value every person brings to the design process and why the ones that will be using a design must be closely involved in creating it. Everyone has their own expertise that can be brought to the design process, so collaborators must ensure together that all voices are heard and valued.

Illustration by Sabrina Dorsainvil

EVERYONE DESIGNS

So what makes a design good for the community? While there are many ways to design for communities, there are some things all community designers should practice. Here is a list of 8 principles derived from interviews with community designers.

Illustration by Sabrina Dorsainvil

 **ESTABLISH TRUST AND BE HONEST**

 **BE PATIENT AND EMPATHIC WITH COMMUNITY MEMBERS**

 **BE FLEXIBLE AND CHALLENGE ANY ASSUMPTIONS YOU MIGHT HAVE HAD COMING IN**

 **BE INCLUSIVE IN ALL ASPECTS OF THE DESIGN PROCESS**

 **LISTEN TO THE COMMUNITY AND VALUE THEIR LIVED EXPERIENCES**

 **BE ACCOUNTABLE TO THE COMMUNITY AND CLEAR ABOUT PROJECT OUTCOMES**

 **DESIGN WITH AND NOT FOR COMMUNITIES**

 **DESIGN IS NOT JUST A CAREER, BUT ALSO A LENS**

PROMPTS

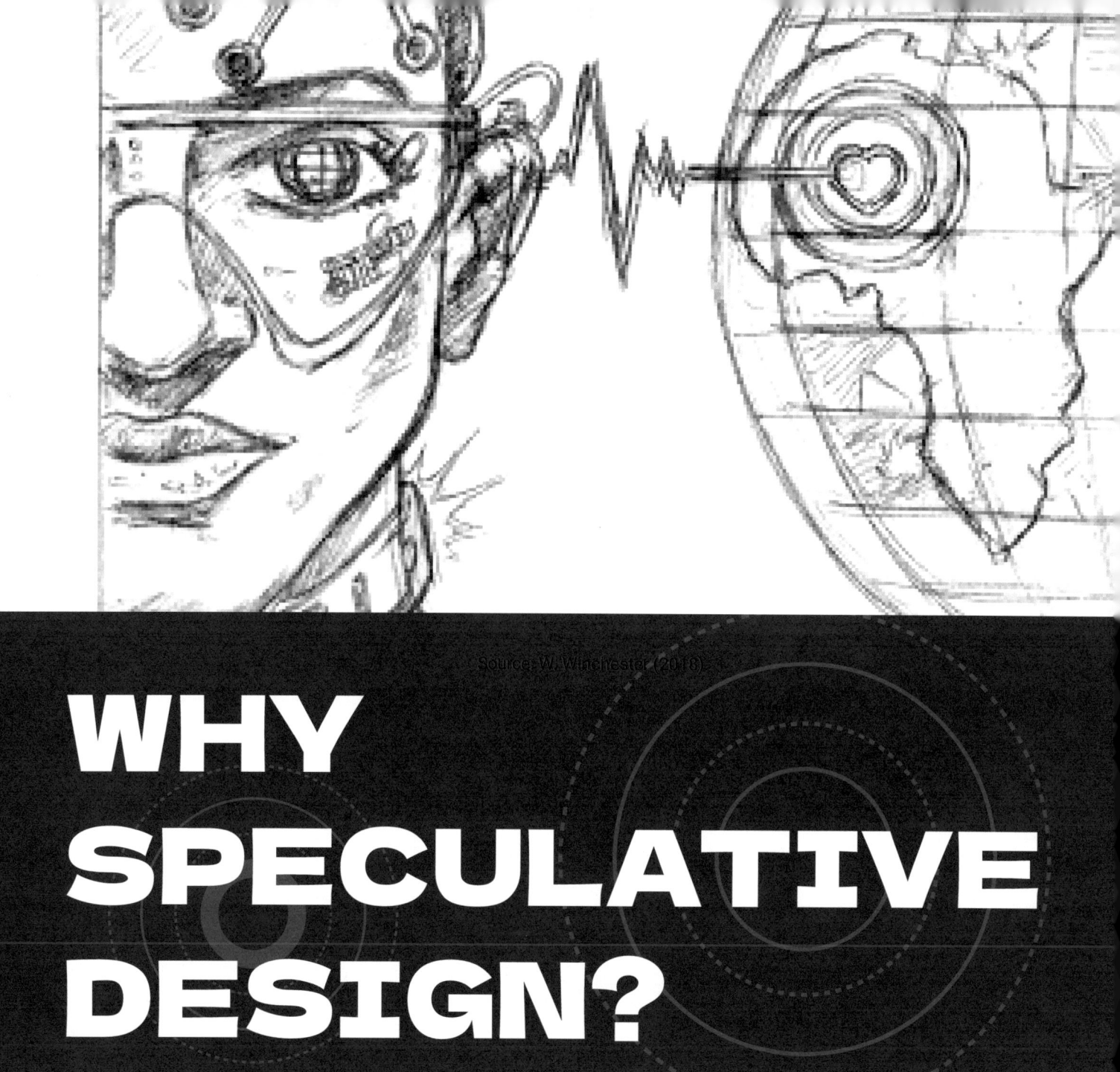

WHY SPECULATIVE DESIGN?

Speculative design is one of many participatory design methods used to help design for the future. The ability to envision is incredibly important and something communities do all the time to consider alternate ways of living. It can help to push us to be more activist in designing solutions for the future that consider both ideal situations and those that negotiate our present-day constraints. On the following pages you'll find prompts to help you begin practicing speculative design.

UTOPIAS

Utopias imagine perfect futures devoid of present-day problems. They are the idealized versions of future worlds and can inspire visions of what the future could be. Is a utopian society possible or desirable? Would a utopia for some be a dystopia for anyone else?

In contrast, dystopias imagine the opposite, showing us failed and broken societies. Dystopias can serve as cautionary tales warning of the outcomes of present-day issues left unresolved. What dystopian themes are in today's society? Are there kinds of dystopias that people presently experience?

DYSTOPIAS

Challenges of our Dystopian Reality

Who experiences a present-day dystopia?
Use this space to sketch or write out dystopian themes you may have seen in today's society.

1

2

3

4

5

6

My Utopian Future

Who is included in your utopia? What does your utopia look like?
Use this space to sketch or write your ideas of what is in your future utopia.

What is possible in your community? What changes will happen there?

_____

_____

_____

_____

_____

_____

_____

_____

 SKETCH OUT YOUR IDEAS. BE AS VISUAL AS POSSIBLE!

WHAT WE SEE FOR OUR COMMUNITY

What is possible in your community?

What changes will happen there?
Which parts will stay the same?

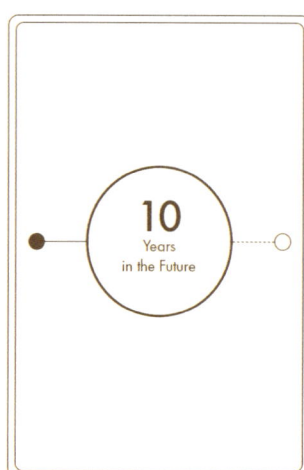

10
Years
in the Future

What I value in my community

What are your community values? How do you support one another?

_____

_____

_____

_____

_____

_____

_____

 SKETCH OUT YOUR IDEAS. BE AS VISUAL AS POSSIBLE!

WHAT I VALUE IN MY COMMUNITY

What are your community values?

Who do you stand up for? How do people in your community support one another?

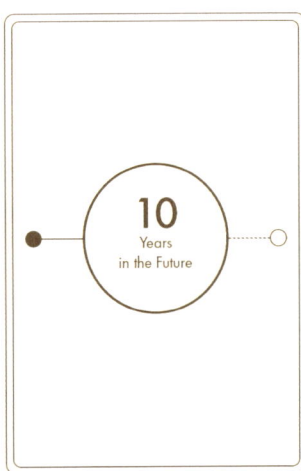

10
Years
in the Future

How I see myself in the future

Where will you be in the future? What will your community look like?

_____

_____

_____

_____

_____

_____

_____

_____

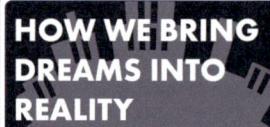 SKETCH OUT YOUR IDEAS. BE AS VISUAL AS POSSIBLE!

HOW WE BRING DREAMS INTO REALITY

What are your dreams for the future?

Reimagining equitable futures can be rooted in the dreams we have for ourselves and our communities. How have you imagined your future? How far or near is that reality? How are you making it real?

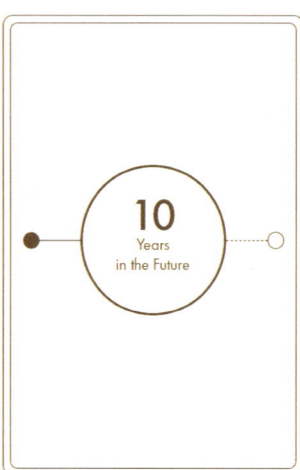

10
Years
in the Future

How should design impact the future?

_____

_____

_____

_____

_____

_____

_____

Scenario

Imagine a scenario where design has changed the future. What changed it? How was a better future created and what does it look like?

_____

_____

_____

_____

_____

_____

DESIGN METHODS

Future Planning

There's more than one way to design your future. Consider the following methods. If one interests you, feel free to take it from the deck and have a closer look. If you have your own methods feel free to use a blank card and add them to the mix!

Concept Scenario

Radical Future Ideation

Collaborative Sketching

Paired Ideation

Future Shaping

Community Conversations

Paper Prototyping

Storyboarding

Open Ideation (Wild Card)

Storyboarding

A storyboard is a great instrument for ideation. In UX design, storyboards shape the user journey and detail how a technology is used. Storyboards help designers to string together user stories and various research findings or insights to develop requirements for the product/technology.

1. Person passing by an advertisement board

2. Notices one announcement and is interested in more information

3. Taking a photo of a barcode on the poster

4. The mobile phone downloads detailed information about the new product.

5. The person puts away the phone and turns around.

Rough sketches capture the gist of the interaction/activity you are trying to depict
Don't worry about getting it perfect. Just make your idea tangible

AN EXAMPLE

1. User arrives at the station and there is a long queue at the ticket office.

2. User goes through application.

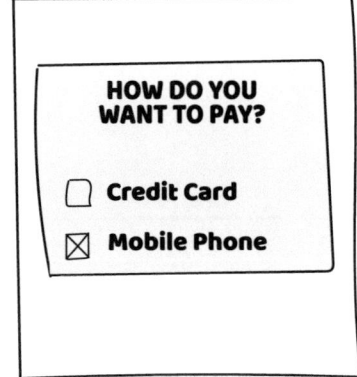

3. On the payment screen, he checks mobile phone.

4. He scans the QR code.

5. Follows instructions and has ticket delivered.

6. Get a train with ticket delivered to your phone.

Storyboarding

There are many solutions you can use to build your utopia. What do your solutions look like? If you're feeling stuck, feel free to pull one of these cards from the Tools & Solutions deck for inspiration.

Data   **Tangible Technology**   **Art**   **Mutual Aid**

Community Projects   **Digital Solutions**

Education   **Community Building**

My Idea

My Idea ⤓

Use the following Building Utopia cards to storyboard ideas for how your community or organization might build something that represents the collective goals of your group.

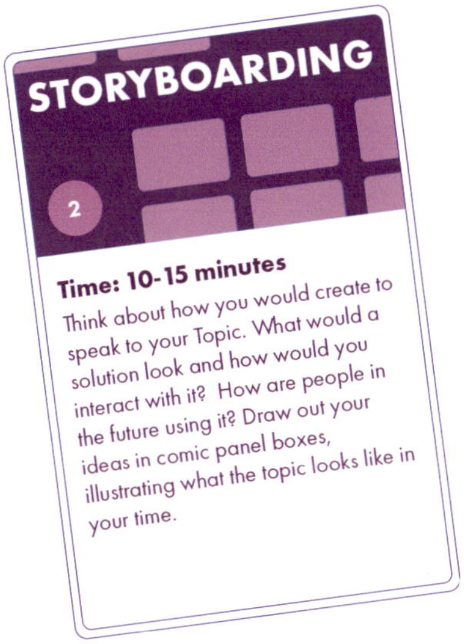

STORYBOARDING

2

Time: 10-15 minutes

Think about how you would create to speak to your Topic. What would a solution look and how would you interact with it? How are people in the future using it? Draw out your ideas in comic panel boxes, illustrating what the topic looks like in your time.

COMMUNITY PROJECTS

Collective goals

Community gardens, installations, or building projects all are ways people can work together and support one another. What community projects are being worked on in your time?

RADICAL FUTURES THINKING

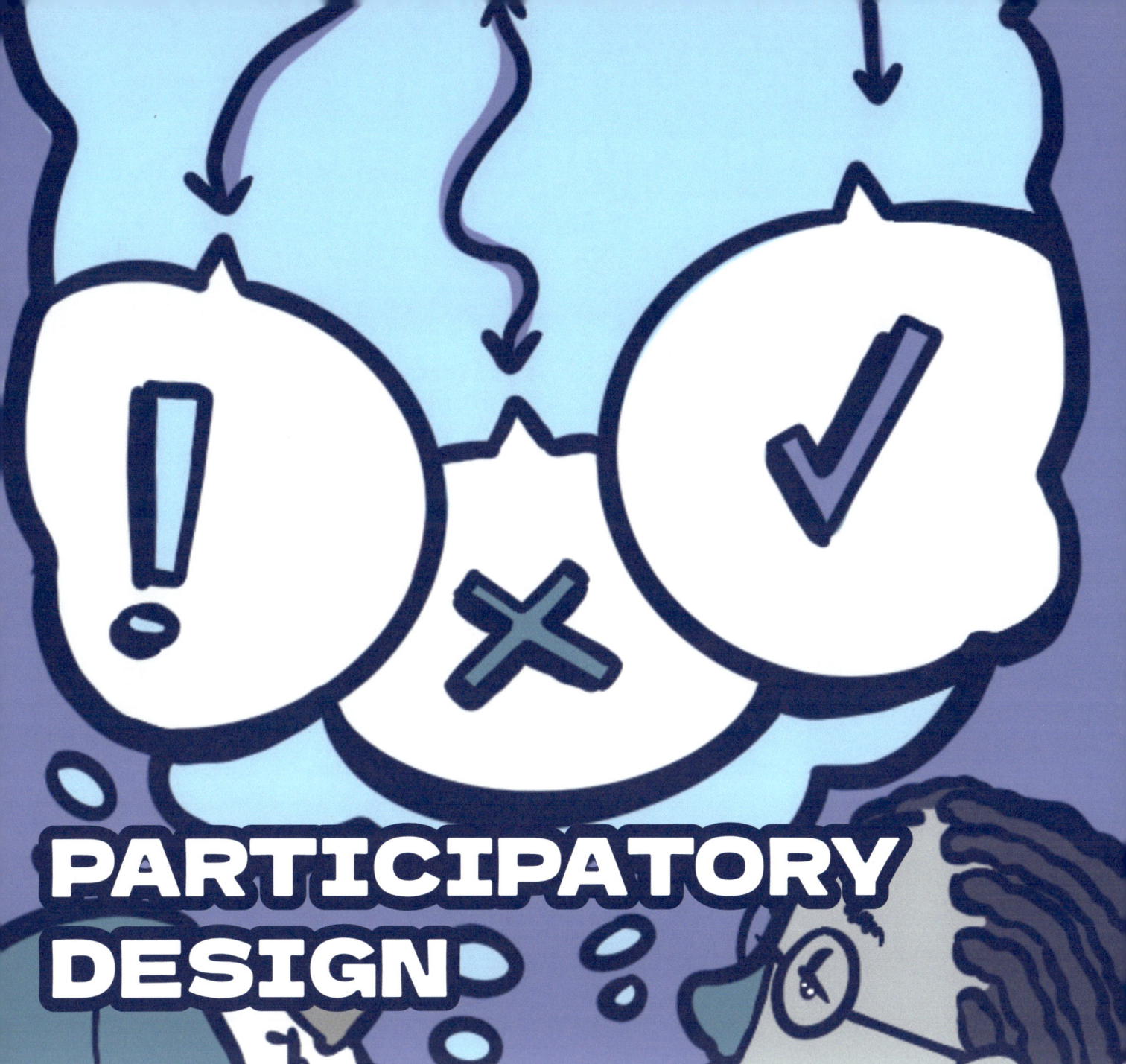

PARTICIPATORY DESIGN

Illustration by Sabrina Dorsainvil

Participatory design brings together groups at all stages of a design. Your voice is valuable in the design process; with or without formal design training, anyone can bring their experiences and personal expertise to the table in participatory design processes. The following pages have suggested pairs of cards to help you begin practicing radical futures thinking with your community.

Radical Futuring: Moments When We Thrive

Imagining the future is a skill we have to practice. There are many ways the future can look if we think collectively and outside of the norm. To get you started, use the two cards paired below, one from the Liberation deck and one from the Methods deck, to imagine what the future could look like for your community in this area. Use the notes and ideation pages to sketch out your ideas.

MOMENTS WHEN WE THRIVE

When are you at your best?

What helps you and your community thrive? Consider the moments when you feel encouraged and recognized.

RADICAL FUTURE IDEATION

Time: 10 minutes

For the next ten minutes, brainstorm a solution without limits or constraints to what currently exists. Here we encourage you to consider radical futures of what could be. Write out solutions as they come to you – no idea is wrong.

IDEATION SHEET

SKETCH OUT YOUR IDEAS. BE AS VISUAL AS POSSIBLE

SKETCH OUT YOUR IDEAS. BE AS VISUAL AS POSSIBLE

Radical Futuring: Moments When I Feel Free

Here's a second pair to try. Use the two cards paired below, one from the Liberation deck and one from the Methods deck, to imagine what the future could look like for your community in this area. Use the notes and ideation pages to sketch out your ideas.

THINKING OF MOMENTS WHEN I FEEL FREE

When do you feel most free?

When are your freest moments?
How do you hold onto that feeling of freedom?

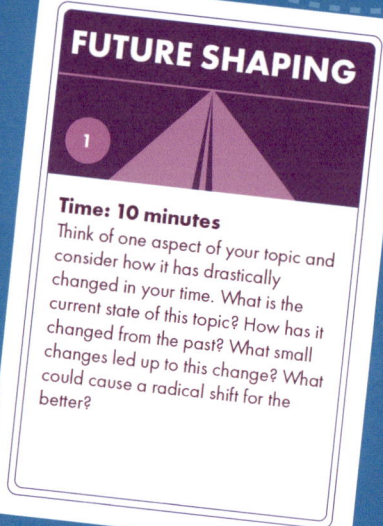

FUTURE SHAPING

1

Time: 10 minutes
Think of one aspect of your topic and consider how it has drastically changed in your time. What is the current state of this topic? How has it changed from the past? What small changes led up to this change? What could cause a radical shift for the better?

_____
_____
_____
_____
_____
_____
_____
_____
_____
_____

IDEATION SHEET

Community Conversations: What are Our Community Values?

Use the Community Values Topics Deck card and the Community Conversations Methods Deck card to discuss what is valued among those with you as a shared community. This exercise can be used at any point in the design or development process as either a way to start a project or as the outcome of community-building.

COMMUNITY VALUES

Shared commitments

Having a set of goals to commit to can help set a vision for what must be done and what has already been achieved. Values can strengthen and unite a community by affirming what is important.

What is valued in your time?
How are these values shown?

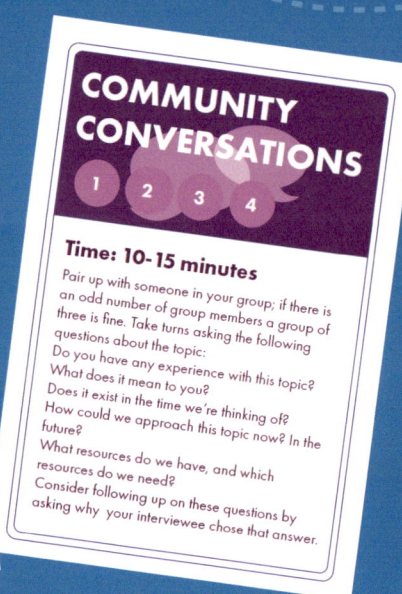

COMMUNITY CONVERSATIONS

1 2 3 4

Time: 10-15 minutes

Pair up with someone in your group; if there is an odd number of group members a group of three is fine. Take turns asking the following questions about the topic:
Do you have any experience with this topic?
What does it mean to you?
Does it exist in the time we're thinking of?
How could we approach this topic now? In the future?
What resources do we have, and which resources do we need?
Consider following up on these questions by asking why your interviewee chose that answer.

_____

_____

_____

_____

_____

_____

_____

_____

_____

Community Brainstorming

What ideas came out of the radical futuring session with your community? Write them out here!

Notes

Notes

DESIGN CONCEPTS

Design Fiction

Design fiction is a design practice aiming at exploring and criticising possible futures by creating speculative, and often provocative, scenarios narrated through designed artifacts.

Speculative Fiction

A broad category of fiction encompassing genres with certain elements that do not exist in the real world, often in the context of supernatural, futuristic or other imaginative themes.

Speculative Design

A design method that addresses societal problems while looking towards the future, and creating designs for those scenarios.

Participatory Design

An approach to design that collaborates with the customers at the core of the design process. This allows the designers a source for a better understanding of their needs.

Co-Design

A design process which allows a wide range of people to make a creative contribution in the formulation and solution of a design problem.

User Experience Design (UX Design)

The process used by design teams to create products that provide meaningful and relevant experiences to the users.

User Interface design (UI Design)

The process designers use to build interfaces in software or computerized devices, while focusing on looks or style. UI design highlights the surface, and overall feel of a design.

User Research/ Design Research

Studies the target users and their needs, to allow designers to have the most precise insights to work with to make the best designs.

Interaction Design

The design of the interaction between the users and the product. The goal is to create these products to enable the users to achieve their objective with the product, in the best way possible.

CONCEPTOS DE DISEÑO

Ficción de diseño

La ficción de diseño es una práctica de diseño destinada a explorar y criticar posibles futuros mediante la creación de escenarios especulativos, y a menudo provocativos, narrados a través de artefactos diseñados.

Ficción especulativa

Una amplia categoría de ficción que abarca géneros con ciertos elementos que no existen en el mundo real, a menudo en el contexto de temas sobrenaturales, futuristas u otros temas imaginativos.

Diseño especulativo

Un método de diseño que aborda los problemas sociales mientras mira hacia el futuro y crea diseños para esos escenarios.

Diseño participativo

Un enfoque de diseño que colabora con los clientes en el núcleo del proceso de diseño. Esto permite a los diseñadores una fuente para una mejor comprensión de sus necesidades.

Co-Diseño

Un proceso de diseño que permite a una amplia gama de personas hacer una contribución creativa en la formulación y solución de un problema de diseño.

Diseño de experiencia de usuario (UX Design)

El proceso utilizado por los equipos de diseño para crear productos que proporcionen experiencias significativas y relevantes a los usuarios.

Diseño de interfaz de usuario (diseño de interfaz de usuario)

El proceso que los diseñadores utilizan para crear interfaces en software o dispositivos computarizados, mientras se centran en el aspecto o el estilo. El diseño de la interfaz de usuario resalta la superficie y la sensación general de un diseño.

Investigación del usuario / Investigación de diseño

Estudia a los usuarios objetivo y sus necesidades para permitir a los diseñadores tener los conocimientos más precisos para hacer los mejores diseños.

Diseño de interacción

El diseño de la interacción entre los usuarios y el producto. El objetivo es crear estos productos para que los usuarios puedan alcanzar su objetivo con el producto en la mejor manera posible.

TECHNOLOGY GLOSSARY

Artificial Intelligence (AI)

A system that is capable of simulating human intelligence. These AI machines are able to learn, reason and act for themselves, and makes their own decisions when faced with new situations.

Internet of Things (IoT)

IoT refers to the connection of devices, including sensors, smartphones, and other wearable devices. Any physical device can be connected to the internet to be controlled, or communicate information, can be an internet of things device. A door lock that can be locked or unlocked using an app on a phone, is an IoT device.

Robotics

Technology that focuses on the design, construction and operation of robots in automation, and can perform tasks that can traditionally be done by humans. Many aspects of robotics involve artificial intelligence.

Machine Learning

Uses AI to allow computers to learn automatically, without intervention or assistance from humans. Machine Learning focuses on the development of computer programs, that can access data and use it to learn for themselves

Autonomous Vehicles

A vehicle that can drive itself from a start point, to its predetermined destination. These are also known as self-driving cars.

Facial Recognition

The ability of a computer to scan, and store human faces for use in verifying or identifying an individual. Facial recognition systems can be used to identify people in photos, video or in real time.

Big Data

Refers to data that is so large, diverse, fast or complex that it continues to grow at increasing rates. Big Data comes from multiple sources and can arrive to the system, in multiple formats.

Data Science

A field of study that combines programming skills, and knowledge of mathematics and statistics to pull meaningful insights from data for the decision-making process.

Cybersecurity

The practice of defending computers, servers, or computer system on the internet from malicious attacks.

GLOSARIO TECNOLÓGICO

Inteligencia artificial (IA)

Un sistema capaz de simular la inteligencia humana. Estas máquinas de IA son capaces de aprender, razonar y actuar por sí mismas, y toma sus propias decisiones cuando se enfrentan a nuevas situaciones.

Internet de las cosas (IoT)

IoT se refiere a la conexión de dispositivos, incluidos sensores, smartphones y otros dispositivos portátiles. Cualquier dispositivo físico puede estar conectado a Internet para ser controlado, o comunicar información, puede ser un dispositivo de Internet de las cosas. Un bloqueo de puerta que se puede bloquear o desbloquear mediante una aplicación de un teléfono es un dispositivo IoT.

Robótica

Tecnología que se centra en el diseño, la construcción y el funcionamiento de robots en la automatización, y puede realizar tareas que tradicionalmente pueden ser realizadas por los seres humanos. Muchos aspectos de la robótica implican inteligencia artificial.

Aprendizaje de máquina

Utiliza la IA para permitir que las computadoras aprendan automáticamente, sin intervención o ayuda de los seres humanos. El aprendizaje automático se centra en el desarrollo de programas informáticos, que pueden acceder a los datos y utilizarlos para aprender por sí mismos.

Vehículos autónomos

Un vehículo que puede conducir desde un punto de partida hasta su destino predeterminado. Estos también se conocen como coches autónomos.

Reconocimiento facial

La capacidad de una computadora para escanear y almacenar caras humanas para su uso en la verificación o identificación de un individuo. Los sistemas de reconocimiento facial se pueden utilizar para identificar a las personas en fotos, vídeos o en tiempo real.

Big Data

Se refiere a datos tan grandes, diversos, rápidos o complejos que siguen creciendo a un ritmo cada vez mayor. Big Data proviene de múltiples fuentes y puede llegar al sistema en múltiples formatos.

Ciencia de datos

Un campo de estudio que combina habilidades de programación y conocimientos de matemáticas y estadísticas para extraer información significativa de los datos para el proceso de toma de decisiones.

Ciberseguridad

La práctica de defender computadoras, servidores o sistemas informáticos en el Internet de ataques maliciosos.

BUILDING

UTOPIA

BUILDINGUTOPIADECK.COM

Made in the USA
Columbia, SC
22 February 2024

32116968R00029